Inner Sanctuary

Words of Wisdom and Guidance

By: Leslie D. Smith

ISBN: 978-1-4404-5553-7

1440455538

Acknowledgements

To my beautiful Children, Hailey and Benjamin: When you came into this world, I was changed. Every day is like a fairy tale with you both! I love you!

To my wonderful husband Don. You have been so supportive of me in all of my endeavors! I love you!

To the many people who have come into my life as teachers. May we all learn from eachother.

Introduction

I decided to put this book together as one more step in my growth process, and with the urging of my wonderfully supportive husband. It contains my personal writings, which include journaling of my thoughts, articles, poems, and channels. My life is in a constant state of change, as is yours, and from the beginning of the writings to the latest writings, I can see how my thoughts have grown and developed. No book written can give you all of the answers that you are seeking, however, books can jumpstart your thinking process. All of the questions that arise within you are already answered for you and by you. You must take the step forward to go within yourself and find them.

Blessings,

Leslie

We Are More Than Our Bodies

Can we mere mortals achieve the stillness to go within and find the answers to the spiritual questions we have within us?

The answer is a loud and resounding yes.

For we are `not' mere mortals, as we have been trained to believe. We have been trained to believe this by our culture, and by our own eyes and other senses. Are we really just a body living life? No, we are not. We are so much more than that. We are spirit. There is no beginning and no end to us. We have created this reality by our own consciousness. We do not have to suffer through life. We do not have to live just to survive. But that is what so many of us do. We do this daily.

You are more than the body that you appear to believe in. It is a trick of the mind. If you could see, for just a moment who you really truly are, you would begin to understand the magnitude of your existence. You are here to spread love and forgiveness; you are here to reach out to others, to help others, to change lives, to help to gently awaken them.

So many are living in a state of denial of their own truth. So many trudge through, with problems crowding their thoughts, worries escalating into anxiety. Fear ridden, they are. This need not be. All of the answers which you seek can be found once you go within, once you find that stillness that is very much a part of you. Within this stillness, there is peace, and there is freedom. Within this stillness, you have an infinite amount of wisdom and knowledge. Within this stillness, you are able to tap into who you really are.

Be still those thoughts in your mind. Many will tell you it is impossible to reach a state of silence. It is not impossible. Nothing is impossible, really.

So many across this planet are waking up, and remembering who they are. So many are searching. This is a joyous occasion.

God

What kinds of thoughts, feelings, or emotions come up when you say or hear this name?

The name of God has been so misused in our history and even today, that I can almost say that it has lost a lot of its meaning. Because of this, many use other names for God, such as Source, Goddess, etc. This is ok. They are all one and the same.

Some equate the name of God with fear, anger, judgment, sin, hell.

Some equate the name of God with Love, peace, tranquility, understanding, freedom.

How do we get such different views?

It depends, to be honest, on how we were raised, and by the life experiences we have gone through up until this point.

God is not a judgmental, fear based, angry, person. These

thoughts about God have come into existence in order to keep people under the thumb of mental hypnotism, in order to keep people encased in a prison of fear. It does not have to be that way, though.

God is not a person. God does not experience any emotions. God does not judge any person or situation. God sees neither good nor bad. God does not see any person as a sinner. God does not understand fear, anger, etc. These have no place in his midst. Those emotions are emotions of the human being. Those emotions are created from our ego-selves. God has nothing to do with them.

God is neither male nor female.

God is the purest expression of Love and Light. We, physical beings, cannot even fathom what this true expression is. We may have glimpses of it every now and then, and when we do, we are sure not to forget the experience. We can, however, when going within and experiencing the stillness of All that Is, begin to remember and awaken to the truth of who we really are. We are a part of this pure expression of love and light.

In my own personal experience, I have become more and more comfortable with using the name of God. It was a long road to get to this place though. Through many experiences and questions, and from going within to the center of my being, I have been taught many wondrous things. Along this path, I have found a peace inside of me. I have found my inner light.

Your Name is Whispered

Your name is whispered

Amongst the billions of stars in the universe

A name not given to you by your earthly parents

But by the Creator

A name so filled with light and sound

You would fall to your face if you heard the sweet, sweet,

sound of it

We whisper this name to you

And it is at these times when you feel the closest to us

You are known by this name

In the world of spirit

And spirit you are, even as you walk this physical plane

You are living in different worlds all at the same time

Love to you

Who Am I?

Have you ever asked yourself this question, 'Who am I?'

Many times, people will answer this question in the following ways: I am (insert name). I am a mother, I am a father, I am a wife, I am a salesperson, I am a daughter, I am a son, I am this, I am that.

Is that who you really are?

Those are labels that you have placed onto yourself, but is that who you really, truly are?

Go deeper with this question. They are three words that can you lead you on an exciting journey.

Who am I?

Eventually, if you continue to peel back the layers of who you identify yourself as, you will come to a place that you can't answer the question any longer. It is a place of nothingness. A place of serenity. A place of peace. Once you find yourself in this place, you will understand who it is you truly are.

Once you have taken all of the worldly identifiers, labels, and your ego out of the equation, you find your real essence.

This place of nothingness, this place of serenity, this place of peace...this is the eternal you. This you never ceases. This you exists even without the body. When you have reached the place where you can answer the question, 'Who Am I?' you will realize you never even had to reach for it, you never even had to strive to find the answer, you never even had to seek to find it. It has always been.

But now, you have just remembered.

Chakra Lesson

Chakra is a Sanskrit word which means 'spinning wheel'.

Our bodies have 7 main chakras, or spinning wheels of energy, which are aligned from the base of the spine to the top of the head. When any of these chakras are blocked in any way, you will have sensations of unrest throughout your body which may manifest as a particular emotion, or even as a physical symptom. Some imagine these to look like a fan with the fan blades rotating, some imagine them to look like the lotus flower, with the petals opening and closing, and some see these chakras as funnels. If you focus your awareness on one of the chakras, you may begin to feel a pulsing sensation, a circular type of movement. Each of the 7 main chakras corresponds to a vibrating color. The easy way to remember the colors is this way, from the bottom and up: ROY G BIV. These are also the colors in the rainbow.

ROOT CHAKRA-The 1st chakra is located at the base of the spine, and its corresponding color is RED. This chakra is said to be related to issues of security, safety, and survival. When one grounds themselves, this is where the grounding stems from.

SACRAL CHAKRA-The 2nd chakra is located between the belly button and the base of the spine, and its corresponding color is ORANGE. This chakra is said to be related to emotion, sexuality, and creative expression.

SOLAR PLEXUS-The 3rd chakra is located at the naval area, and its corresponding color is YELLOW. This chakra is said to be related to energy, assimilation, and digestion.

HEART CHAKRA-The 4th chakra is located in the center of your chest, and its corresponding color is GREEN. This chakra is said to be related to love, balance, and well-being.

THROAT CHAKRA-The 5th chakra is located in the throat, and its corresponding color is BLUE. This chakra is said to be the point of communication and growth as a form of expression.

THIRD EYE/BROW CHAKRA-The 6th chakra is located in the middle of your forehead, and its corresponding color is

INDIGO. This chakra is said to be the sight of psychic awareness.

CROWN CHAKRA-The 7th chakra is located at the top of your head, and its corresponding color is either VIOLET or WHITE. This chakra is said to be the point of divine consciousness, the master chakra which controls all of the others.

Chakra's are not seen with the physical eyes, but can be felt, as they are aspects of consciousness, however, you can feel how these chakras relate to you and how you are feeling at any given moment if you place your awareness on what is going on in your physical body, and with your emotions. Basically, you can tell what chakras are blocked by what is going on with yourself if you become more aware.

All bodies have these 7 main chakras, it's a part of the divine vital life force which runs through us at all times. We also have many minor chakras, to name a couple; we also have ear chakras, which are located at a diagonal position right above our ears. We also have chakras in each of our fingertips and in the palms of our hands.

CHAKRA BREATH EXERCISE

There is a technique one can do to help to energize the entire
chakra system, and clear blockages. The below technique
works for me. However, keep in mind, that that are many
different ways to do this, and finding the one that works for
you is most important. My experiences will not be yours.

Find a place where you can be relaxed. You can either sit or lie
down for this, as long as you have a quiet place with no
interruptions. Turn off the phone, and let others know that this
is 'your' time.

Don't worry about the thoughts running around in your mind.
This technique will have you focusing your awareness on
specific energy centers, the 7 main chakras within your body,
which means that most thoughts will be on the back burner.

So, get in your comfortable position, and just begin breathing.
Let your belly expand with each breath.

After a few breaths, focus on the bottom of your spine, or your
tailbone area. Imagine a ball (about the size of a cd disc) in that

area. See this ball glowing with a bright red color. Watch this ball of red light. In your visualization, you may see that the ball is darker in some places, you may notice movement. Breathe. Imagine your breath as white light and breathe INTO the red ball. See this red ball illuminated with the white light. Breathe out through your mouth, and exhale away any impurities. Just see them flow out of your body with each breath. Keep breathing white light into the red ball. This is your **ROOT chakra**, and helps to cleanse it, open it up, all allow the energies to flow through with every inhale, and the impurities and flow out with every exhale.

Once you feel good about your ROOT Chakra, move on to your SACRAL chakra.

You will use the same visualization as above for every chakra point.

For your **Sacral Chakra**, see this as a ball of Orange glowing light. This is located between your naval and your root chakra.

Next, move to your **Solar Plexus Chakra**. See this is a ball of

Yellow glowing light. This is located at your belly button.

Move to your **Heart Chakra**. See this as a ball of Green glowing light. This is located in the center of your chest.

Move to your **Throat Chakra**. See this as a ball of Blue glowing light. This is located at the center of your throat.

Move to your **Brow/Third Eye Chakra**. See this as a ball of Indigo glowing light. This is located in the center of your forehead.

Finally, move to your **Crown Chakra**. This one will be different from the others. See this chakra as a funnel shape. The smaller part of the funnel going into the top of your head, and the larger part of the funnel extending outwards. Breathe in white light into the funnel, and exhale through your mouth a few times. Then, breathe in again through this funnel, and imagine your breath as the white light. Have this white light travel down through each of your other chakras.

Note how you feel after this exercise.

Human Be-ing

Human Being.

Ponder on those two words for a moment. Human~you. Being.

What does it mean to just Be.

We have heard many times through our lives, just be who you are. However, we have also taken that to mean something different than what it really is. 'Don't worry about it, just be who you are'. I bet that at some point in your life, you took that as a call to your ego, to stand up for who you are on a surface level.

I ask you to go deeper with being who you are. From the very essence, from your very core, can you be who you are?

You Are Not Alone

One of the strongest feelings you may experience when you realize you have begun to 'Awaken', is the feeling of being alone.

You may feel as if the things that once meant so much to you are now meaningless when looking through your new found eyes. You may feel that you don't connect as well as you did with those you have known for so very long. When you are Awakening, you come to realize that you are essentially formless, you come to realize that you no longer identify with those things in the material world which once were so important to you, you come to realize that all along, YOU have been right here, and had placed meaning where meaning wasn't to be found.

What is happening is that your ego is dis-identifying with your mind. You have been such a part of the ego, and the ego has been such a part of you, that a piece of you is mourning the loss.

When one begins to feel lost and alone, remember that you are not. There are many others on the same path. You are beginning to peel away the layers of who you truly are, and you feel a sense of separation. You are being separated from your ego-self. Your ego-self is a part of the mind that seeks to control who you are.

We are not separate from anything. In all things, we are one. We are all part of Consciousness.

Change

There is a widely used phrase that goes like this. "Life sucks."

Life does not suck. It is the view you hold within your mind that determines how you see life. This view can be skewed by many outside factors, many situations that appear externally. In turn, you let the negative influx of thoughts and emotions run rampant until you can expend no more energy and then ultimately, you give up. You have lost all energy. When it gets to this point, one says…"life sucks."

This does not have to be. You can, and do have the ability within you to transform the way you see things. You have the ability to become more aware of what is going on internally as far as thoughts go and the way you act or react to the emotions which are running through you.

You can become the observer in any situation.

You can step back and change the way you look at people, things, and situations.

When you become aware of this process and find that you can do this, it appears that people are changing for the better, it appears that situations which you have labeled as 'bad' in the past, are now turning into 'good' situations, or that things are changing in positive ways. However, it is not the external factors that are changing at all. It is the internal and eternal YOU which has transformed all of these things.

It is you who is changing.

Row, Row, Row Your Boat

Row Row Row your boat, gently down the stream, merrily, merrily, merrily, merrily, Life is but a dream.

We used to sing that song as children, and children still sing it today.

I've never really thought about the song much until a few months ago. I was driving home from work, and I just started singing it, absent mindedly. Then it dawned on me that I was singing it in my car, and loud too…and then I began to sing it with mindfulness, and paid attention to each and every word, singing very slowly.

What a very inspirational and powerful message this little song holds within it.

Row, row, row your boat, gently down the stream: We need to move through life (our boat), gently.

If we force ourselves to do things in a hurried like motion, if we force ourselves to do things which cause stress, if we force ourselves to do things that we really dislike doing, then we are no longer moving through life gently. When we do let go a little bit, if we allow things to happen, and just move down the stream of life, gently, things begin to fall into place, effortlessly. We find that when we allow, and when we surrender, we realize that we never had to push so hard in the first place. This doesn't mean to just sit there and wait for things to happen. This means that we still use our oars, we just move more gently.

Merrily, merrily, merrily, merrily: Happiness. Need I say more? We don't have to go out looking for happiness. Happiness is already there.

Life is but a dream: Ah yes, one of those things that one could write a book upon. We consciously and sometimes subconsciously create everything within our lives. Everything we see, touch, feel, hear, sense. We have created it all.

Keep rowing, gently, happily, life is but a dream.

Keep on Going

Overwhelmed?

Little things can begin as little things, and then all of a sudden all of these little things pile on top of each other, and once this happens, one can feel overwhelmed by all of the things that they need to get done. In this case, it becomes anxiety and panic.

My advice to those that come to me who are in this situation is to start very small. If needed, make a list of all of these little things that need to be done.

Start with the first thing on the list. Don't do anything else. Just complete the first little thing. Mark it off of your list, and move on to the next one. Keep going!

When I was a little girl, my room when get so full of mess. I'd have stuff in every corner, and under my bed, didn't even want to open my closet because it was so messy. My mom would make me sit in there and clean it for a whole day. I remember being in there sitting on the middle of my floor, and I was just crying. I was so overwhelmed, thinking I'd never get anything done. I felt like my world was falling in on me, over a room! of all things. So I'd have to start in one corner and just clean that corner, and then move over a little bit, and clean that, and so on and so forth. Just by seeing the progress I made in one spot, gave me the push to keep going.

Keep on going!

Be-ing in the Present

What's it like to be in the present moment?

To me, it has created space. It has created freedom.

Being, in my past, a very anxious type of person, who worried about things that had already happened, and worried about things that had not happened yet, it seemed that I was constantly living either, in the past, or in the future, but never in this very moment.

I began to focus on my center. I literally focused in the middle of my chest, my heart center. I began to breathe deeply through that space. When a worry would arise, I would observe that thought, and then move past it, and re-focus myself to what I was doing 'right now'.

I saw the results of doing this, when I knew something important was coming up. I decided I would begin to live 'in the now'. I decided I would become aware, that I would be present. When that date finally arrived, there was no nervous tension, there was no anxiety, and I felt as free as a bird. That important thing came and went peacefully.

It takes a re-training of the mind, to get to this place. But it can happen. And it has for me. I am free, and I can breathe easily.

Where Am I?

The other night, as I lay down to sleep, I had this question running through my head. Had lots of thoughts running through my head, but this one was the loudest. If this body is the vehicle for my spirit, and what a precious vehicle it is, then where am I in this? I've touched on this briefly before, questioning myself, but it seemed that this particular night, something really wanted me to explore this. Where am I in this precious vehicle of expression?

I practice being aware, being centered. But when I'm practicing that, as I should always be...where am I? Is there a place inside that I am? Is there a place outside that I am?

Knowing that we are all part of the Whole, and experiencing it are two different things. I have experienced in a few occasions, but in very quick spurts.

So, again, Where Am I, really?

And Spirit answers: "I AM in every breath. I AM in every cell of your being. I AM within and without. I AM internal and external. I AM everywhere, all at once."

The Great Dream

Who are you? The answer is really just a breath away.

If you could, come and travel with me for a moment, into a Great Dream. In this dream, you can be whoever you want to be. In this dream, you can do whatever you want to do. In this dream, you can create whatever you want to create. In this dream, there are endless possibilities. In this dream, your thoughts can manifest into being. In this dream, you are in a state of joy and of peace. In this dream, you have no limits!

Now wouldn't that be completely mind-blowing? Wouldn't that be fabulous??

What if I told you that you are, right now, in this Great Dream? What if I told you that the words you are reading right now are part of your dream, that your family and friends are part of your dream, that your job is part of your dream, and so on and so forth?

Yes. This is your Great Dream. Really! You have created it. You will continue to create it, except for one thing. Sometimes you forget. You forget that it's a grand illusion! You forget that you don't have to fear anything. To be in fear, is the biggest thing that is holding you back from creating the life that you really want. The only reason you aren't creating what you want, is that you are afraid of something. What is it? What are you afraid of? I'm sure you have a list a mile long. What if you could just throw that list away? Would you feel freedom? Would you feel at peace if you could do that?

You have nothing to fear in this Great Dream. Nothing can harm you, take anything away from you, or destroy you, really, in this Great Dream. Now, while you are in this Great Dream, there will be many opportunities for you to fall into the trap of fear. While you are here though, you can work on erasing it; you can work on feeling free. Free is what you are.

Realize that you are a wondrous beautiful being of pure Light. Realize that you are here to experience, to create. Realize that everything you do is experienced by God.

How is that? That is so because God is not some elusive character living up in the sky, separate from you. God is inside of you. God is inside of me. God is inside of your children. God is inside of your neighbor, and your dog, and your cat, and inside of everything. God is able to experience everything through you. You are completely Divine.

You, god, are experiencing The Great Dream!

You are LimitLESS

Limit your thoughts and beliefs, and you have thus limited yourself.

When you place these lines around yourself, never daring to color outside of them, you have boxed yourself into limitedness.

However, you are LIMITLESS. If you do not allow yourself to be as you are, you will have a limited view of yourself, others, and life itself.

When you can become aware, when you can become the Vessel of Love that you truly are, the lines begin to disappear, you begin to see other dimensions, other realities, other paths, becoming more and more open to All That Is.

When you can be one with Limitlessness, you will begin to sense things with your Spiritual Senses, instead of with the senses of the Physical Body. When you are able to see God in yourself, in others, in all life, your life here expands into greater possibilities.

You are Unlimited. You are able, you have, and you are allowed to create that which you want to create.

Do not live in fear of what you think you don't have, what you think you need, what you think others think of you, what you think is coming down the road. Do not fear what is on the Other Side of this physical life. Many falsities have been spread through the ages to keep you inside of this fear, to keep you inside of this box, for the purpose of limiting YOU.

Gently awaken, dear ones, to the knowledge of who you are. This knowledge you can find by silencing yourself, by asking yourself the great questions, by not fearing the answers you are given from yourself.

This is where you will find great wisdom. This is where you will find YOU. Listen.

CREATE or CANCEL

Funny thing I wanted to share with you.

When I went to write something for this blog, it asked me to
choose a document made from a template or a blank document.
I CHOSE blank document. It then gave me a choice to
CREATE or CANCEL.

Right then and there, my blog entry started to form. What an
inspiration! We CHOOSE to CREATE or to CANCEL
everything, at every second. We are the creators of our lives, of
every experience that we have, or rather, that we CHOOSE to
have. We bring people in, we bring situations in. We'd like to
believe that we don't, because we don't want to blame
ourselves for THAT, we would rather blame it on someone
else. Right? But the cold hard truth is, it's YOU. It's ME. WE
create all of those things, every single one of them! This then
leads us down the path of 'Victimville'. We can no longer be
victims of our past experiences, can we?

If you are really open, if you really just 'allow' yourself to BE,
without asking how, without asking why, without knowing

what is going to happen, then you will begin to see transformations in your life. Divine Inspirations begin to come to you. Allow yourself to act on these Divine Inspirations, without questioning it and there will be ease.

Choose to Allow. Choose to not have to know the answer to why? Or how? Or when? Or what? When you Allow, you put trust in the Divine. When you question, you have begun to block out the Divine Inspiration.

Miraculous

Miraculous.

To be alive at this time in history.

To be here, to be breathing, to be experiencing. What a miraculous time this is!

To open up to the knowledge, to the knowing, to the remembering of WHO we really ARE!

To see so many people opening up, to see so many people awakening to the TRUTH, absolutely beautiful!

This is the time of magic and miracles!

I am completely exhilarated with the knowing that I CHOSE to be here at this time, with YOU!

Transformation Through Self Talk

I have realized that when we begin to talk to ourselves, out loud, that we can have some really transforming moments. There was a time when I would be embarrassed to even SING in my car if I was alone, for fear that others would see me and think I was crazy. Oh, I've come a long way baby!

What makes us so different from those who we label as 'crazy' anyways? We see people talking to themselves on the street as they walk along, and say or think, 'man, they must be crazy!' And then we walk or drive along with thousand of thoughts of our own running through our heads, a lot of them not so sane! What if we said all of them out loud? Would we not then be 'crazy' as well? There's just the matter of saying them out loud, or letting them roll through your mind!

Anyhow, I was driving home from work yesterday, and began talking, out loud, to myself. I was thinking about negativity. Everyone always says, be positive, push the negative thoughts out of your mind. So as I was talking to myself, I began to channel my higher self, and began speaking, to me. :)

In that conversation, I was told that negativity is not necessarily a bad thing, at least, in those who begin to realize that they don't want to live a negative life. When one is being negative, critical, or anything which is not in alignment with the essence of love, the essence of joy, one can know that their energy is not flowing in the way in which it should. One can know that something is stuck. Just by identifying that you are being in a false state of mind, you then begin to open yourself up, you begin to clear away that stuck energy. If one can identify and then choose to clear themselves, the liquid flow of light begins to stream through your body once again.

One "Peace"

I have, over the past couple of years, been thinking quite extensively on the subject of peace.

When someone asks what my biggest wish would be, I really do respond with "World Peace." It sounds so flaky, and maybe a little crazy, but it's the truth.

How do we get to that point? One "peace" at a time. First, the peace from within. We cannot have peace in the external world, if we ourselves do not first see the peace within us. We must first change ourselves, on an inner level, if we hope to make a change elsewhere.

There are many that would say there is no way to achieve World Peace. Well, maybe we can't achieve it in this lifetime we are currently living, but if we get the ball rolling, in our future lifetimes here on earth, it is a real possibility. I believe that all things are possible.

We can spread our Peace within to the outside world by our thoughts, by our actions. One little "peace" at a time, given from many different people, can really add up to a wondrous result!

Spread it with a smile, spread it with a laugh, spread it by listening to another, spread it by helping those less fortunate, spread it by giving, spread it by being of service to another~just for the mere joy of giving.

The Crystallized Mind

Many individuals walk around with crystallized minds. To be in this particular state of mind, one has closed off all doors. These individuals walk around with their minds set for life. There is nothing that they question, because in truth, to question anything would mean possibility of a change within themselves or those around them. Fear is what holds back the crystallized mind. Fear is the biggest obstacle one can face in this life. I would venture to say that Fear constitutes pretty much everything we encounter that holds us back. Fear of death, fear of poverty, fear of flying, fear of public speaking, fear of losing someone we love, and the list goes on and on.

So how does one go about releasing this crystallization? Firstly, one must want it to be released. From there on out, the crystals begin to fall off, one by one.

If one dares to begin to ask themselves questions that they never wanted to ask themselves, such as: 'Who am I really?', 'Where did I really come from?', 'What is Life, anyway?', then, loads of crystals will begin to be released.

Once just one crystal begins to fall away, therein lies a clear light, a light that begins to shine on something you never thought you would begin to see. Changes within yourself begin to take place. You notice that your mind becomes more open, you begin to feel and taste what freedom is and means to you. You begin to find your Truth.

However, many individuals feel safe in the environment of the crystallized mind. Nothing changes, nothing moves, and fear has become their comfort.

It is a choice one must make. Live in fear, or live in Truth. To each choice, is a lesson to be learned.

The Mind

I have come to realize, through my inner studies, as well as my semi-outer studies that Meditation, or self-hypnosis, hypnotherapy, and dream journaling can be extremely to helpful in one's daily life.

First, a little bit of knowledge about our minds: Our conscious minds make up 12% of our minds at any one time. It is responsible for our current awareness and decision making. Your subconscious mind makes up 88% of your mind. This subconscious part of our minds is where our personality is derived from, where you store your feelings and your thoughts, where you memory bank sits. This includes all of your morals and values, beliefs, and habits, all of your 'programming'. The way that one reacts in their waking state, is normally created by pulling out ("automatically") things from our memory banks. Once we are overloaded with information, we get very tired, we get stressed, and we can get easily irritated. This is where sleep is very important.

In our dream states, we are able to release, or rather, vent, a lot of what is going on in our subconscious minds. This dream state helps us to release stress, and work out problems on another level of consciousness. It essentially, makes more room. If one was not able to dream, one would literally go crazy. If you would like to have more knowledge of what you are dreaming about, it would be extremely helpful to keep a pad of paper and pen next to you as you sleep. Upon awakening, immediately write down any symbols or images you have seen, any conversations, events, anything you can remember. If you wake up several times in the middle of the night, do this as well. Don't think that you can just wait until 'later' to do this. You'll probably forget a lot of pertinent information. It will go back down into your subconscious mind. By doing this, you will begin to see that your dreams do hold messages for you.

You can also release, or vent, in a state of meditation, as well as self-hypnosis.

When you are in a deep state of meditation, your brain waves begin to slow down, causing a dream like state. When in meditation, you are able to access super-conscious levels of your mind, where you can also receive information, intuition, creative intelligence, be ONE with your Higher-Self, your God-Mind, etc. . It is in this super-conscious state where many people get their great ideas, where they are first formed. It is in this super-conscious state where you find your True Self.

Self-Hypnosis and Meditation can be related in some ways. Hypnosis can be used as a tool for relaxation and stress relief, as well as re-programming one's mind with positive thoughts, ergo, affirmations, and this can also be done in Meditation. Meditation is a place where one is able to go into a deeper state of Oneness, a deeper state of Being.

There is also hetero-hypnosis, which is where one uses a Hypnotherapist. There are several myths about Hypnosis in general, some being that you are asleep, or that you will lose all control and your Hypnotherapist can control you from there. This is not the case. Hypnosis is a great tool to look into. You are never 'asleep' in the sense of what sleep means. You are always aware of what is going on, and if you are also always in control. If there is a suggestion made that you do not like, you don't have to accept it. You are never at any time put under a 'spell'. The Hypnotherapist can guide you into several different states of hypnosis, and can program your sub-conscious mind to receive positive messages, or affirmations, therefore, beginning the process of re-programming your mind. The Hypnotherapist can take you into a deep trance state as well, and in this place, you can also access your super conscious mind. With self-hypnosis, you aren't really able to get yourself into a trance state...you would just eventually fall asleep.

We can all re-program ourselves, our ways of thinking. We can all access our inner selves, our True Wisdom, our God-Minds. We no longer need to re-act to situations in the way we once did. We can truly change the way we do things, if we so wish. We are unlimited. The only thing that keeps us where we are is Homeostasis. Homeostasis is a resistance to change. It will do its best to keep you still, keep you from moving ahead. Fight that homeostasis within yourself.

You Are Worthy

Have you ever been asked this question in an interview, or while answering questions on some different test?

1. How do you see yourself?
2. How do others see you?

In a way, both of those questions are important. On the other hand, the second question is irrelevant, because every individual will see what they want to see in a person, they will have their own perception, and from different angles. However, that second question is the one most people ask themselves on a daily basis, and this question alone can cause someone to become embarrassed easily, can cause them to hide themselves behind others for fear of how others see them, and can even cause an irrational sense of low self esteem.

Most importantly, how do you see yourself? Make a list. Be honest. If you find that you see something in yourself that you do not particularly care for, set about to make a change, now.

I'm here to tell you that what you think of yourself is the most important. You ARE the most important person in your life. Spending time with yourself, and spending time being positive about yourself, and doing things for yourself, is above all else, the most important thing in your life. I know to some that it may seem like a selfish thing to say, but if you let yourself go, and you let yourself feel not worthy, then nothing else in your life is going to feel good to you. You must make the time to spend on you.

I myself fell into the trap of always doing things for other people. I felt like I had the weight of the world on my shoulders, that I had to be the one that took care of everything, because people expected me to. It was my job as a mother, as a wife, as a friend. But I could see that it was taking its toll on me. It was only when I surrendered this part of myself, that the weight was lifted, that I felt freedom for the first time. Guess what? My kids, my husband, and my friends were all fine. I don't stop caring for my family and friends, and I don't stop doing the things that I want to do, but I did stop doing the things that I did not want to do. I did stop taking their feelings as my own, and worrying so much about everything.

Many of you are 'yes' people. You just can't say no to anyone, and there are different reasons for this. One being that you want to please other people, and you want them to be happy, you don't want to let them down. Another being that you don't want other people to see you as someone who won't lend a hand. You are worried about what they will think of you if you say no. Some people say 'yes' from a genuine standpoint, but there is a fine line between doing something because you want to, and because other people want you to. Only say yes if it makes you feel good. Only say yes because you want to say yes.

If you are a 'yes' person, and you are feeling the stress from this, please begin to take the time to look at yourself, and spend time on yourself. Do NOT feel guilty for making yourself happy. You are worthy of happiness, you are worthy of feeling good, you are worthy, period!

God, Source, Spirit, whatever you wish to call this force that is you, does not wish for you to be in a state of anything but love. When you feel down, you can know that there is something that needs to be changed. The only one that can change this is you. You are a very powerful person. You can do things that you probably don't even know you can do, because you haven't tried. You've put yourself on the back burner. It is time to put yourself at the head of the line. Take care of yourself first, and then others. It is not selfish. It is how you were meant to be.

Addicted to Drama?

Do you think that you are addicted to drama?

Sometimes we are attracted to pain and suffering, the drama's in our lives. This is something that we learn from an early age. And while, when we were young, the first time we suffered it was probably shocking, and very hurtful, we then became used to this feeling of pain. We can become attracted to the drama in life because it is comforting. We can become addicted to pain, believe it or not. I know it sounds crazy, suffering as comfort, but the truth of the matter is that when we become comfortable with something, we strive to continue in this comfort, painful as it can be, subconsciously. If there is not drama in our lives, we look for it, we wonder why the drama is gone, and then cannot continue on until we find it. We can become depressed and anxious if there is no drama. Drama is a drug.

When we are content, we begin to stir things up. Something must be wrong if things feel content. Right?

To become free from the drama, we must become observant in all things that we do. We must become observant on the things which we think, the things that we feel, the things that we say, the things which we respond to. BE-come the observer, the witness, instead of the participant.

Strive to let go of the drama, the addiction to pain and suffering. You are not meant to live in a state of pain and suffering. Such trickery you have been led into, but you can lead yourself out of it.

Begin today.

Voices From The Light #2 - 25-June-2008

Voices From The Light – Channeled by Leslie Smith 25-June-2008

Blessed are you who are fearful. Blessed are you who hold fear in the palm of your hand. What shall you do with this fear? You may either take it into your being, or you may transmute this fear into love. For fear is a necessary component in the life of duality. It is what it is. We observe, and we walk with you, in your daily lives, and we see this fear. Observe it. Look at it from the real you. The real you is not your skin. The real you is not your eyes. The real you is not your fingers, your arms, or your breath. The real you is not your brain. Look at it with the eyes of wisdom, which is the essence of who you are. When you can sense, when you can feel this fear from the observing view point, you are able to transmute this fear, love it, and let it go. Fear is an all powerful, draining type of energy that is able to paralyze you into a state of submission. Allow the fear to come, observe, hold it, and surrender it.

Blessed equally are those who are unable to transmute this fear. We take you into our hands, metaphorically, and blow the sweet winds of love into your lives.

We Are One in This Together

To everyone that I know in this life
To all of you that I've known in others
To all living beings which walk through this life
We are one in this together
The pasts that we've had have been gifts
Sometimes in disguise
Yet beautiful all the same
The present moments that we share
Are amazing
And the futures will be so as well
We are one in this together
As we join hands
And travel together through our lives
May we each see the beauty in each other
May we no longer judge
May we see with our inner vision
The splendor before us and behind us
We are one in this together

Choose Gratitude

How many of you have no problems to face in your life? How
many of you go about your day and everything is fabulous,
wonderful, happiness and joy 24-7?
I don't see any hands raised.

We all have issues to face every day. It is how we look at them
that determines how we will experience our day.

So my friend, we'll call her Kathy, woke up late today. Her
alarm went off, but she kept hitting the snooze button. How
many of us do this on a daily basis? I know I do. Because of
this, she started her day late, and because she got up late, she
was already in panic mode, already in a state of anxiety,
already worried about walking through the door at work and
getting the evil eye from her boss. She felt this way all the way
to work. When she got to work, indeed, the evil eye was given
to her, and because of this, she felt bad the entire day. Every
little thing annoyed her, she took comments made to her in a
pessimistic way, she snapped at her co-workers, and she had a
headache. What happened in this day to create such a problem?
Some would say the whole idea that she set her alarm on

snooze started it all.

Now let's change Kathy's story a little bit.

So my friend, we'll call her Kathy, woke up late today. Her
alarm went off, but she kept hitting the snooze button. Instead
of getting into panic mode, instead of becoming anxious, and
instead of becoming worried about what her boss may think,
she went into a state of gratitude. She thanked Spirit for the
beautiful day that was given to her, she thanked Spirit for
allowing her the extra sleep that she had needed so much. She
thanked Spirit for the life she had been given. She decided that
she would have a wonderful day today. On the way to work,
she called her boss, and let him know that she would be a little
late, and was told that it was no problem. She arrived at work
in a good mood, and decided that she would stay in a good
mood for the rest of the day. She saw each moment as a gift.
What happened in this day that caused her to flow so easily?

Choice happened.

She chose gratitude, and she chose to create her day in the way she wanted it to be created.

When we are in a state of gratitude, we have naturally uplifted ourselves, and we have put forth the intent for the high vibrations to flow through quite easily.

We can make this choice on a daily basis. Which is easier, which seems more uplifting?

Choose gratitude.

Raising a Child of Light

Never Demand Respect

I know that you may have grown up with parents who demanded your respect. You may have been expected to be seen and not heard. I know it sounds crazy to say to 'never demand respect' from your children. The truth of the matter is if you demand respect, you will never truly receive respect. If you really wish for your children to respect you, then you must also show respect to your children. Believe it or not, respect is earned. As an adult, you would never respect someone who demanded it from you. However, if someone showed respect to you by 'being' respectful in all ways toward you, most likely, you would reciprocate. The same rule applies with children. Children are not toys; children are not robots. Children are people.

Never hit your child in a state of Anger

Before I had children, I decided I would never hit my children - period. This is a personal decision for each parent, and I will explain why I chose to not do this. I have learned that if you hit a child, the child is more likely to respond by hitting others. I have learned that violence breeds more violence. I choose to raise my child in an environment of love. Spanking a child can be done with love as long as it is never, ever done while you are angry. There are indeed differences when someone hits their child when angry, or when they do it out of discipline. Punishment and discipline are very different. A child can sense the differences. Children are people.

Trust your child

If you can show that you have trust in your child, then your child will be trustworthy. Your child will trust you.

Respect Your Child's Privacy

As you need your privacy, your child also needs their privacy. There are some parents that feel the need to look over their child's shoulder at everything that they are doing. There are some parents who go through their child's things without the child's knowledge. There are some parents who won't let their children out of their sight. If you are an involved parent (which is the way to be) then your child should be well versed on the dangers of the Internet, of speaking with strangers, of sex, of the dangers of drugs and alcohol, and so on. Just to clarify about the Internet, if a child has issues with following the rules of being on the computer, should be placed in a place where the family gathers. If you suffocate your child, most likely your child will do whatever it takes to get more breathing room, and that means the child may actually begin to try and hide things, where if they had been given a sense of privacy, they probably wouldn't have. Children are people.

Get involved

If you aren't already involved in your child's life, then start now. Be involved in their education, be involved with their homework, be involved with who are their friends, and be involved in knowing their likes and dislikes. Be involved, and be interested. Children are people.

Talk with your child

If you keep the dialogue open between your children and

yourself, you will find that they will come to you first if they need something. If they trust you, and respect you (see above), they will find your guidance important to them. If you are able to talk with your child openly without judging them, you will know if there is some sort of behavior (i.e. depression) or any other mood differences that signify that there has been a change in your child. Children, just as adults, are prone to depression, low self esteem, etc. Children are people.

Be open Spiritually

Never dismiss a child's spirituality. Children come into this world with spiritual knowledge. It is only when this knowledge is dismissed as fantasy or imagination that the child begins to lock it all away. If your child has an imaginary friend, it's OKAY. It's not crazy. If a child sees angels, then ask them what they look like! Don't tell them they're just making it up, or to stop. Nurture your child's spirituality. Teach them LOVE. When you teach them love, they will show love to themselves and others. Children are people.

Don't sweat the Small Stuff

Don't buy the expensive shoes for your children if they like to get out in nature and get dirty. Children love to explore, and being allowed to explore should be nurtured.

If they spill their drink at the dinner table, let them know it's an easy clean-up job. After all, we've all spilled our drink before. If they've left their toys out, instead of getting angry, let them know it would help you out very much if they cleaned those up for you. Children actually like to be helpful.

Watch them intently

When you watch your child, see their innocence. Watch them play, watch what they create, watch how they think, and watch what they say. It may amaze you to see how they grow, and how you can grow just by watching. Children are people

Keep your promises

Never make a promise to your child that you cannot keep. A promise is something of importance to a child, so, if you think you may not be able to do something, then do not make a promise. Children are people.

Hold a Vision of your child

Instead of complaining about your child about what a mess they make all the time, that they are troublemakers, that they never listen to you, that they don't respect you, etc., hold a different vision of your child in your mind. See them as perfect (because they are), see them as loving, see them as special. When you change the vision you have of them in your mind, then you actually change what you see in them. Children are people.

Love your children.

Reclaim Your Life!

There is much to be said about those who are living the role of 'victim' at this time. Maybe you have been playing this part for quite some time. Maybe you have been hurt over and over again in this life, and all you feel like saying is ''Why me?''.

Why do we have to suffer? Most of us have gone through some things we can label as pretty terrible. Some of us are going through these things right now. We may not be able to see over the hill that leads to freedom from whatever we feel is weighing us down, whatever we feel may be keeping us from the life that we want to live. We may blame this on our parents, our other relatives, or the relationships we have gone through or are currently going through. We may blame it on our jobs, our bosses, our employees, and the list could go on and on for days.

What I'm about to say will be the first time hearing it for some people. And for others, you are coming to, or have already come to this realization.

You and you alone, are holding yourself back from living the life you dream of.

You do not have to be the victim any longer, unless you choose to be. If you haven't read my blog called 'The Greatest Gift', I encourage you to go and read through it right now.

You and you alone, are responsible for the life you are leading today. You and you alone are the Creator of your life.

You hold within yourself a very powerful force. There is no time to blame others for where you are standing today. There is no time to say 'poor me' anymore. It is now time to stand up, and re-claim your life. Begin today! Use this time, and use this moment, to make a choice. Don't let other people that have been in your life, and that are in your life today, create your life for you! When you let others create your life, you have given your power away! When your thoughts linger in the past, and you find yourself mulling over something someone said that caused you pain, or if you feel like getting back at them, you have stepped down into a lower vibration, a negative thought pattern. When you do this, you have given your power away!

Your Spirit, above all else, calls to you. Spirit whispers in your ear. Have you paid attention to the whispers? Spirit tells you that you are magnetic. Whatever thoughts you are holding will attract more of the same to you. Spirit says that you are Precious and Perfect. Open your eyes and make the choice to create your life the way you want it to be.

Reclaim your life!

Voices From the Light #1

Voices From The Light ~ Channeled by Leslie Smith on 19-June-2008

Beyond the mind which you have limited yourself to, is something far greater than you had ever dreamed of. Beyond the mind, is pure Consciousness.

If you tap into this universal energy, your questions and answers are there all at once. You will see that you can do more things than you ever thought were possible, by letting go of old belief systems. In fact, you must let go of 'all' belief systems. Holding on to any one belief system is a way of limiting yourself. You then place yourself inside of a comfy box.

There are so many things that you do not know, and do not grasp at this time, and until you become pure consciousness without form, you will not know. We like to see this energy that is pouring forth right now. The light that is exuding from those of you on Planet Gaia is bright. Every time someone awakens, the light becomes brighter. Every time you hold the vibration of light in your mind, the light grows. While there is much darkness on the Earth which you walk upon, there is also much light. The switch has been flicked to the 'on' position. When this happens , the darkness begins to fade way.

Do not ever feel like your 'little light' as many of you call it, can't do anything. One light means all the difference. Mother Earth is not the only living organism which you are affecting. There are many planets, many universes, galaxies..ALL is affected. Consciousness rises. Consciousness uplifts. Consciousness vibrates at a powerful speed.

We thank you. We know this is not an easy path to walk upon, and we are gracious that you accept this position with gratitude. We know that this path can be a lonely one at times, and we are gracious that you still walk it.

We are among you, and we observe, and we see all that is going on. But do not let any of your daily troubles, your worries, cloud what is the Truth of All.

See beyond them, keep moving. The energy is in a constant state of change. There is never stagnation.

Do not let your thoughts be fixated on the darkness that is in your world at this time. To do so only attracts more thoughts of the like. You need not have those worries. All is happening exactly as it is meant to happen.

All that is happening is perfect, and wondrous. Be grateful every day. Wear a smile on your face. Wear your heart on your sleeve. See peace.

Live peace. We are One.

Connections

Have we sacrificed our connections to each other? Have we lost the ability to connect with each other, and with all of nature, and with the Earth, Gaia? Perhaps we have done this, through time. We can see that those of us in modern society use material possessions to fill that connection. We want the best house, the best car, the 'things' that we feel connect us to humanity. Mostly, what these things do is connect us even closer to our ego's, making us feel somehow higher than others, and we keep acquiring more and more possessions, in order to keep climbing the ego ladder. What we find then, is that we never have enough, and it's a never ending cycle.

Take a look at those who do not live in modern society. Let's look at those tribes of people all over the world who do not have this type of need to fill their lives with 'things'. What are they connected to? They are deeply connected with the other humans in their tribes, they are deeply connected to the Earth, and many have a deep sense of intuition that they use to guide them in their daily lives.

Now for the What If's:

What if we stopped the constant feeding of our ego's? What if we put away the greed, the jealousy, the anger, the "FEAR"? What if we decided to share with others in a sense that they were all family members? What if we allowed our hearts to expand in such a way that our eyes became fresh and new? What if when we let go of all the meaning that material items seem to give to us, we then began to connect with each other in a new, deeper way? What if we honored the Earth for all that she has given to us? What if we could see that the Earth is indeed a living Being?

We are beginning to do this. We are beginning to shift into a way of living, of being, that has not been before seen on this cycle of the Earth, and the Earth has had many cycles, many renewals. We are awakening to the Consciousness. We are integrating ourselves to be out of the mind, and walking into something new. More and more of us are becoming aware, and when the consciousness of the planet evolves and lifts to a higher vibration, it begins to shift even those who were asleep.

Let our hearts expand, and let us hold each other's hands as we walk towards the beginning of something spectacular!

Encouragement

How often have you thought about someone and thought something really positive about them? Sometimes, the thought is so strong, it makes you smile, and you have this overwhelming urge to let it out! This could be the person sitting next to you, a friend, or even the cashier at the grocery store. Now how often have you voiced that thought, sitting in your head, to that person? And how many opportunities have you let slip by you because you have thought too much about that thought, and overanalyzed it, and eventually decided it was better NOT to voice it?! Isn't it funny how we can do that?

I have found that even the person who seems to be having the grumpiest day in the world, can completely change their attitude when someone says something nice to them, or when someone just gives them a smile. It can actually make their whole day brighter. This is because the vibrations that we carry with us, when they are positive in nature, are seemingly flowing through us to that person. Sometimes, it is enough to just sit next them, and sometimes, we need to let those words of encouragement come out of our mouths. We need to trust our inner guidance on this one. When I say inner guidance I'm not speaking of the overanalyzing of our thoughts, that is a completely different thing. Inner guidance comes from the heart center.

I know that we've all heard this story before, and many times, we hear it, and it passes right through, but I am encouraging YOU to make a difference in someone's life TODAY!

The Boy and The Well

The boy went to the well every day, to see if there was water there. There was no reason to go to the well other than out of plain curiosity and something to do. Even when it rained, the well remained empty. He would drop a rock into the well every day, and hear it make a clinking noise onto the ground. It made no sense. Until one day, he grew so tired with the well, he decided once and for all to ask the well to fill with water. As soon as he asked this, he heard a noise, and it sounded like the rushing of water. He grabbed a rock, and threw it down into the well. Sure enough, there was a splash. After a few moments, the well was filled with water. His mouth was open in awe. He looked into the magical pool, and saw his own reflection. He put his hand into the water to make sure it was real, and he swooshed his fingers around and around. After a while, still amazed, he left for the day. The next day, the well was empty again. He frowned, but then he had remembered something. He had asked the well to fill with water yesterday, so he decided to try it again. Sure enough, the well filled with water again. He smiled to himself, realizing that all he needed to do was ask. So simple.

Although this is a metaphoric story, it is a great reminder to those of us who sometimes don't ask for what we want in this life. Sometimes what we ask for may not be given to us in the way that we wish it would, but if we pay attention, what we ask for is 'always' given to us in some form or another. We only have to be awake and pay attention, and always, remember the magic of asking.

The Greatest Gift

Many fear that which they do not understand. It is part of being human. But we can go beyond this fear with introspection.

You can look up anything these days on the internet, and see positive attributes of a thing, or negative attributes of a thing. For example, you can look up any religion, and see good things said about it, and then turn around and see bad things said about it. You can look up the word 'energy' and see good things said about it, and then turn around and see bad things said about it. You can look up 'peace' and the same thing happens. This goes for all things. But you must not accept all things as they are said to you, you must not accept all things as your own just because you have heard them from someone else, just because they have been written by what appears to be an authority.

One of my favorite quotes is a quote from Buddha, and I share this quote daily with those who ask me questions about their own lives.

Buddha said:

"Do not believe in anything simply because you have heard it.
Do not believe in traditions because they have been handed
down for many generations. Do not believe anything because it
is spoken and rumored by many. Do not believe in anything
because it is written in your religious books. Do not believe in
anything merely on the authority of your teachers and elders.
But after observation and analysis, when you find that anything
agrees with reason and is conducive to the good and the benefit
of one and all, then accept it and live up to it."

Each person must use their own inner discernment.

How does one do that?

You must go back to the very beginning. This isn't about living
in the past. This is about getting rid of the past that doesn't
belong with you any longer. This is about becoming aware of
and beginning to live your life from a new perspective. This is
about being in the now moment, about living in the present.

You must, with your own mind, go through from your earliest memories, which can be a long and painstaking task, and you must go through each one and look at the filters that you have agreed to accept. Put aside all of the false beliefs that you may have acquired through your life. You must look to yourself and literally feel what is right for you, what spells out T-R-U-T-H to you. When you do this, you will find that there are many things that you decided long ago to let slide by, to not question, and these things then became a part of your life. You must look to the judgments that you have agreed to accept about yourself and others in the past. You will find that there were and still are many situations in which you decided to become a 'victim' because of certain beliefs that you held to be true.

When you use your inner discernment, which is one of the greatest tools we have available for our use, you will begin to change yourself, and you will begin to change how you look at things. Things that caused you grief in the past will eventually pass away. You will begin to understand things from a place of truth, instead a place of false beliefs.

You must then begin a process of forgiveness; forgiveness of yourself, forgiveness of others in your past and in your present, forgiveness of situations, etc. This process of forgiveness will be an ongoing process that will need to be done in your daily life. You will find an inner peace, an inner sanctuary that is being cleared away for new growth.

You will find that as you go through this process, weight is seemingly lifted off of your shoulders, physical pains will be released from your body, and a new outlook on life will begin to emerge.

This, you will find, will be the greatest gift that you could ever receive; a gift that you give to yourself.

The Wind

I dream of one day being the wind
Free, unassuming, unaffected
Flowing wherever it wishes to
Traveling across the entire world
Swaying with every leaf on every tree
meandering through every blade of grass
Tip toeing across the waters of every ocean, every lake, every
river, every pond
Blowing gently across a person's face
Tickling the toes of a baby's foot
As I stand upon my own two feet
My dream becomes realized
I become a part of the wind that journeys through life
In this space of the present moment

Love In Any Language

Last week, I was speaking with a friend about traveling to other countries (Haiti and Mexico) when I was a teenager, and having the opportunity to meet with children in orphanages. It was said that we went there to 'work' in the orphanages, but that is not what it was for me. It was never work. I was 15 years old when I went to Haiti for 2 weeks during the summer. This trip would be my most memorable. We were to go there and 'work' with the children. Actually, I remember mostly speaking with children, and adults alike. I remember walking through the markets, and learning about their land, listening to their stories, and I remember loving these people from a distant land.

When our plane first landed in Port-Au-Prince, I got my taste of what a third world country was. All of these people were crowding the landing area, to see who was getting off of the plane. I think I probably should have been afraid, but I wasn't. As we boarded the small van for the 3 hour drive to our destination, I realized the drive would be longer than I thought. Driving on a small dirt road, very bumpy, we came across many groups of police that would stop people as they went by and go through their things. Luckily, this did not happen to us on the way there. As we drove, there would be small dirt and grass huts along the way, children running around naked, with distended bellies from mal nutrition, and I remember seeing one woman lying on her porch. They said that she had AIDS. I was so sad to see all of this, and what a wake-up call it was for a 15 year old girl from America.

In Haiti, they speak French and Creole. I had a little book of words to say and learn. I only learned one. It was 'Bonswa'. It was what you would say to say "hello", and also to say "good-bye". Turned out, that would be the only word that I would ever need to know while I was there. We had a Haitian translator that went with us everywhere, and we all became quite close to him. His name was Firmin. He was in his early 20's, and he had dreams of becoming a Doctor and moving to America when he was able to. He told us many stories, and seemed to keep us out of harm's way. I never knew what happened to him when we left Haiti.

While we were there, I realized that all of the children we met were very smiley, very sweet, very happy precious children.

The adults were the same way. They were helpful, always wanted to talk to us, teach us songs, and befriended us. I could not help but to have my heart strings pulled this way and that.

Again, I only knew the word 'Bonswa', and they didn't know English either. But, there was no language barrier. We didn't need to know each other's language. I saw these people from Haiti as my brothers and my sisters. When we wanted to convey things to each other, we would convey it with our eyes, we would convey it by using our hands to draw symbols in the air, or with our fingers, drawing something in the dirt. We would convey things by giving hugs. We would convey through our hearts.

The most important thing I took from that trip was that we are all brothers and sisters. It doesn't matter where we live, what color our skin is, what kind of financial situation we are in, what language we speak.

With love, and through our hearts, we are all connected. The gifts that we give to each other are seeing past all of those things that try to separate us from each other, and realizing that there is no separation.

Here I AM

Whispers
Riding the streaming light of the breeze
Speaking to you softly
Brushing across your cheek
Ever so gently
Saying "Here I AM"
Scents
Of a nearby blooming flower
The petals so fragile, so beautiful
Saying "Here I AM"
Droplets
Of dew upon a green blade of grass
Twinkling in the morning light
Saying "Here I AM"
Music
That the birds sing to eachother
And to you
Saying "Here I AM"
Here I AM, Here I AM, Here I AM
Are you listening, are you watching
Are you Present?

Voices From The Light #4

Within is the stillness, the stillness that most humans do not take the time to connect with. There is a place where you can go to connect with the stillness. This is like connecting to shall we say Ameren UE or to whatever big power company you use..this is like plugging in and receiving electricity. When you go to this place of stillness, you are truly connecting with Creatorship, the Divine You. To not plug in is to deplete your soul to the point of wariness. You need not go through rituals to plug in. You need only to be still. You need only to focus on centeredness. It is ok for thoughts to run rampant at this time. You will find that as you let them run wildly, and not engage them, they will get bored with you, and you will be left in a place of quietness. While in this quietness, there will be a magnitude of love that perhaps you had not known before. You have of course, always known it, but while in form, and while driving yourself crazy in stressful situations that take over your mind in this game of life…maybe you have not allowed yourself this experience of Absolute Oneness. Perhaps you have caught glimpses of it. Perhaps you will find that you will choose to plug in more often. That is what the meaning of 'within' is. When someone chooses to tell you to look within yourself for the answers, you now know what they are speaking of.

Voices From The Light #3

Channeled by Leslie Smith on 22-July-2008

You never needed to be here! You've already ascended! You are a master! Each and every one of you! You CHOSE to come here, many have chosen to come here time after time, some have chosen to go to other dimensions. YET, this has been a choice of yours, a choice that you have made. While here you have forgotten the ways of peace. But you are remembering. It has always been this way. You come here, you forget, you remember, you leave, you come back. You do this for the experience. You do this to learn. You do this for the joy of it. How can you do something like this, you ask of yourself. Why would I ever choose to come here and experience this pain over and over again? Because your soul knows that it is not painful. Your soul knows that it's an illusion, one that you could instantly leave if you wished to do so. It's not a bad thing to be inside of the illusion. For you are also outside of the illusion. You are in all places at once. Your Higher Self, which is not in the human way 'higher' but has all remembrance..is always watching, always observing, always directing you. You are in the hands of safety at all times. Do not judge your time here as bad or as good. It is only different. In an instant, you could gather yourself up and take your place outside of the illusion. You choose not to at this time. You have things that you wish to experience, things that can only be experienced while in form. But be not fooled into thinking that you are form itself. This is one of those things that happens quite often. You can be tricked, you can be fooled in the ways of this world. But we are here to tell you to be not fooled into thinking you are form itself. You are not to be contained only in this seemingly real physical form. You are limitless. You have to make the choice to see it though. You have the free will. You have designed yourself this way. To connect with the Self of All Remembrance, is your way of putting the pieces together. We will be speaking with you frequently. Do not fret. However, do not hold things within. To have emotion is not good or bad. Do not judge it. Just let the emotions come, let them flow. If you let them get stuck, there is nowhere for them to go. Let them move THROUGH you, be not stuck INSIDE of you. Mmm, Indeed we see your questions. Indeed we know what is happening in your mind.

Ah, the mind of all minds, that processing magnet of thoughts. We see that you have been 'stuck' on certain questions, which we know that in this transmission, we have relieved. Keep moving. Yet stay still. Be still.

Take Off The Mask

Do not hide behind a mask. You created this mask as you grew older, and the mask changes depending on where you are at the moment. The mask brings comfort to hide the pain inside. The mask hides who you really are! You do not need the mask, you only think you do. What would happen if you took it off for a moment? Do you think you could do it?

Let me tell you something, you were not given this life to hide. You did not choose this life so that you could be someone or something that you are not.

You did not come here to be small. You chose to come here to experience. You chose to come here to live.

You, in all of your wondrous being, are brighter than the Sun. But you have forgotten that!

Start remembering.

Take the mask off. Try it. The real you deserves to be shown to the world!

The Match

Do not follow me. Just let me point you to a path. There are many paths. You choose which way you wish to go. Do you know how to choose? There is no wrong path, although some may seem easier than others. Let your heart choose for you, not your head. Take this lamp. Let it light your way for you. If the flame blows out, use this match to light it again. This one match will work every time you use it. The light may blow out often. If you stumble, get back up again, and keep walking. Don't try to walk the path in darkness, there is no need. Just remember…. the match.

The Call

When that phone rings, are you going to pick it up, or let it go to voice mail, perhaps getting lost in the shuffle?

We are being called ladies and gentlemen, boys and girls. We are being called by Truth.

You can feel it within the depths of your inner being. You can feel it in your bones. You can feel it pulsing through you. You can see it in the outer world, and you can see it in the inner world.

There is a great sense that you must find your place in this world. There is a great sense that there is something more out there. The riddle in there is that there is no place in this physical world, and there is nothing out there that is going to quench your thirst. There is no book and there is no teacher that can give you the answers to the questions you have. These things can surely guide you, but you will find that still, you have unanswered questions.

You see, you must live in this world and at the same time, not be a part of it. If you become a part of this world, you lose the sense of who you really are. If you mold yourself into the puzzle of the outer world, you have lost your way. You must live here in this physical place, and it can be a struggle. No one said it would be easy, did they? When you answer the call from Truth, and surrender everything you thought you knew, Truth will be your guiding path. There is not one way to the Truth, there are many paths. However, there is only ONE Truth.

When you answer the call of Truth, you will begin to hear Truth telling you that you have already found your place, that it never went anywhere. Truth will tell you that there is nothing out there that will satisfy you. Truth will tell you that the greatest teacher is your Divine Self. You are the Divine Self, in every way.

Make no mistake, Truth is not 'out there' somewhere. Truth is not wrapped up in a guru. Truth is not waiting at the end of the road for you to come and find it.

You are Truth. Everything you have ever searched for is right before you. When you answer the call from Truth, you will be speaking to your Self.

Sleeping While You're Awake

Sleeping while you're awake.

What does that mean?

There are some of you who know what I'm talking about. I've been asleep while to all outside appearances I was wide awake. For me, this means that it looks like someone is fully awake. After all, they are functioning in the world like they are supposed to. They are breathing. They do all the normal things you do in life. Yet, they are still sleeping.

There are a number of things that can happen in life that begin to awaken someone. You may have gone through a terrible relationship, you may have had an out of body experience, you may have died and come back to life, you may had a stressful illness, or it may happen not from anything out of the ordinary at all, it may just be that you read something, or that you wake up one day and things are different.
To begin to awaken from this slumber means that you are beginning to see the world a little differently, maybe a LOT differently. I'm going to make a list of 'may happen' things.

'May happen' things are things that 'may happen' when you begin to awaken. Not everyone will experience the same thing. But I have found that many DO experience similar things.

You may:

1. Begin to see the same numbers over and over again. For example, a big one is 11:11 or 444 or 777.

2. Begin to hear guidance from a voice within your head that seems quite
positive, something you've never heard before.

3. Begin to pick up creative abilities that you've never used before.

4. Begin to start reading everything you can on Spiritual subjects.

5. Begin to question the religion you have been a part of.

6. Begin to lose interest in things that used to interest you.

7. Begin to feel that the things that you own are just things, they don't really matter any longer.

8. Begin to question why everyone seems so materialistic.

9. Begin to pick up abilities such as energy healing, seeing/feelings spirits, a knowing of things.

10. Begin to feel more compassionate towards others.

11. Begin to lose the judgment of others that you once found yourself engaged in.

12. Begin to feel like all things are connected in some way.

13. Begin to lose interest in the life you had before you began to awaken.

14. Begin to feel as if you are supposed to be doing something meaningful, but you don't know what it is.

15. Begin to open up emotionally, crying sometimes for no reason.

16. Begin to feel alone.

17. And the list goes on....

All of these things that you 'may' experience are very normal once the alarm clock sounds. You will be awakening for a long time. You will not be fully awake until you make the transition from this physical body into the world of Spirit. You are a spirit with a physical body, not a physical body with a spirit.

The best advice is for you to find a group of people that you can share these things with, and there are a lot of groups like this popping up all over the world. Many people are beginning to awaken. Some have been awakening for decades. You are not alone in this. You are never alone.

It is not recommended while you are awakening for you get in other people's faces and try to wake them up as well. This won't work, and is not suggested. Not all people who are on the earth at this time are going to hear the alarm clock ringing. Some may hear it and press the snooze button, and will drift back into their slumber. Some will wake right up! Whether they awaken or not, it's ok. You placed this alarm onto your path. Perhaps you placed alarms all along your path. Sometimes, you have passed right by the alarm. This time, you chose to listen to it. You chose to stand up from the slumber, to see what was going on.

Your Amazing Dreams

No matter what life you were born into, whether you be rich or poor, no matter the color of your skin, no matter where you live, you have had at one time in your life or another, a dream. Sometimes, we have many of them going on all at one time. I'm not speaking of the kind of dreams that you have as you fall deep into REM sleep. I'm talking about the dreams that come from the very core of your soul. I'm talking about those dreams that you have for yourself, for your life, for your future. Dreams are built upon passion. Passion comes from your Spirit.

Do you remember being a child? As children, we love to explore different things. Everything is brand new. Everything is a discovery. Ask any child that you know about his or her dreams, what he or she wants to be in this life, and I bet you that without hesitation, they will have an answer for you. They are filled with wide eyed wonderment and excitement. They are absolutely, positively 100% sure of these dreams that they share with you. Their dreams can change on a daily basis, or even minute by minute. One minute they may want to be a superhero, the other a race car driver. One minute they may want to be a princess, and the other, an artist. Children have no fear of anything because it hasn't been instilled into them at this point.

Then something happens. Inevitably, at one point or another, as we continue to grow older, there will be someone who laughs at those dreams, someone who tells us it is not possible, someone who tries to take that dream away from us, be it a person that you know or don't know, by your living circumstances, or even by watching something on television. Some of us are fortunate to have people in their lives as we grow up that try to keep these dreams alive. A lot of us though, fall into a trap that we didn't know was there in the first place. It is the trap of fear. Fear is thrown at us from every direction. Our minds accept these ideas of fear, become used to these ideas of fear, and we begin to live our lives worrying about what will happen next, what won't happen next, what if I'm not good enough to do that, and the list of fear-based thoughts could go on for miles.

Our dreams though, even if there are now cracks in them, are still always there, sneaking up on us, shaking us up, and trying to get us back up on our feet. When we really have something that we are passionate about, we are filled with excitement.

The fear can easily set in. Fear is a roadblock. Fear wants you to stay put. Fear is afraid of any kind of movement, and kind of change. But you can overcome this. You can erase this fear with one word. That word is 'Choice'. Yes, it may seem tough, but it is a lot easier than you may think. Choose to follow that dream, whatever it may be. Don't listen to the Fear, no matter where or whom it is coming from. Choose to CANCEL the fear.

You are stronger that you imagine yourself to be, and you can overcome whatever fear you have that is blocking the path for you. When you choose to cancel the fear, you will see that the path has been cleared away. You can breathe again. You can take a step forward now, towards that amazing dream of yours.

See The Now

"There will be time to do that later. " "I will do that after I get this done." " Maybe later I will (fill in the blank).""As soon as I finish (fill in the blank), THEN, I can (fill in the blank)."

How many things are you putting off for a later time, a later date? How many strings do you have that are untied? How many things that are important to you, are you putting on the back burner, and what is it that is putting them there?

There is only the present moment. There is only now. The only sure thing in this physical life is now. There is no past, because it is now gone. There is no future, because it hasn't arrived. But there is always right now.

While you are here on this earth, you are here to experience. If you do not experience, then what else are you doing? What kinds of experiences are you having? What are the most important things in your life? Who are the most important people in your life?

Take the time now, in this very moment, to stop putting things off for 'later'. Do not miss out on opportunities that come your way for growth of the Spirit, of Your Spirit. Sometimes we even miss messages meant for us, because we are not paying attention. Begin to pay attention to the NOW.

This isn't a message based on fear. This isn't a message to tell you that you don't have much time. But it is a message to let you know that this physical life is indeed short. This is a message to let you know that there may be things in this particular life that you are to take part in, and make peace with. This is all a part of growth. There is indeed a reason that you are here on this planet, right now. What is the reason?

This life has been given to you as a gift. Take care of yourself NOW. See the gift that has been given to you. See the endless chances that you have now to experience truth, love, peace, and light. See the NOW at every second.

Emerge Anew

Has there ever been something going on within your life in which you say over and over to yourself, and sometimes even complain out loud to others, 'Why Me? What did I do to deserve this?'

Has there ever been an obstacle put in your path, and you just fell to the floor distraught, not knowing what to do about it? Has there ever been anything that happened that you thought you would never ever get through?

Did you eventually get through it? How did you do it? Are you still stuck inside of something and don't know how to get out?

I know that I personally have had my fair share of troubles, blocks, and train wrecks thrown at me. At the time during which these things had their place in my life, my outlook on things was entirely different, however, they shaped the person that I am today, and I would not be where I am right now without them. I truly believe that weakness can make you stronger. When you really feel like you are dry of hope, when you fall to the ground in anguish, when you heart hurts and you can't take it anymore, that is the moment in which you can rise up and become strong.

During my younger years, up until I was 30, I felt like I had trouble after trouble haunting me. I felt as if I must have done something awfully wrong in a past life to get me to this point, because no matter where I turned, something sprouted up to block my way. Something always seemed to be there, waiting for me to have a moment of calm in my life, just so it could disrupt that feeling. I felt as if I must be the most unlucky person in the world. If the straws were to be picked, I always got the short one. Little did I know, that those things were shaping me into the strong woman that I am today. Little did I know that by getting through those things, it has led me here. Little did I know that I would die at the age of 30 and be re-born into someone completely new.

Die? How did you die, you are still here? Many of you may be questioning.

I died not of a physical death, but a death of the old me. Funny, because all while I was growing up, I really did fear turning the age of 30, as I thought I would die before that day arrived.

How true it was indeed! My old self died, and the new me emerged into life.

I began to see that I was responsible for absolutely everything in my life that I had been thrown. Absolutely everything! I had no reason to ask why me, I had no reason to blame others any longer. I was not the victim, except of my own thoughts. My thoughts had victimized me, and yet, I was responsible for being the victim. No longer would I allow that to enter into my frame of reference. No longer would I ever see others the same way. No longer would I allow myself to fall into the trap of self-pity. Many people do not understand the thought process here. They ask, how can you be to blame for (insert thing here)? Well, the truth of the matter is, I have created this life of mine. I have the free will to be, do, and act as I choose. If I choose to be the victim, then I am creating a story for myself that I do not like. If I choose to be free from victimization, then I am creating for myself a great novel! By taking the responsibility of all things that occur in my life, I know that I can change them to be any way that I wish for them to be!

When things come my way, I can go back to those times in which I was the weakest, and draw upon my own strength, the strength that the Holy Spirit has instilled into my life. When I am walking hand in hand with the Holy Spirit, I am being guided with peace, with love, and with life.

Breaking Free

Breaking free from societal viewpoints and beliefs, which are oft considered the blueprint or rulebook on how to live your life, is not an easy thing to consider, but if you are worn out from not following your own truth, know that it is time to make a new choice. When you break free from what is considered the normal practices, and listen more to what your own Self is saying to you, when you follow how your own Self is directing you, when you, with intent follow the directions in which your heart is leading you, you will find unceasing joy and fulfillment.

Perhaps you have been on the same road for a long time now, trying to fit in, trying to adjust to your environment, trying to make everyone happy, every one that is, but yourself. Maybe you are just now noticing that you are not happy with the way things are traveling.

This is a pivotal point in your life. You can now choose to keep driving along this same road of life, or you can choose to take the exit onto another road. If you choose the other road, there will always be more roads to choose from.

You must follow the path in which your heart leads you.

The hardest choices to make are usually the most necessary.

Cultivate leadership within yourself. Sow the seeds of freedom within yourself. Do not look unto others to find great spiritual meaning. Look within yourself first and foremost.

Break Free.

Voices From The Light #6

channeled by Leslie Smith on 9/24/08

You are always in the Holy Presence of Now. You always have been and you always will be. You are standing on Holy Ground right now. But, many of you do not recognize this Holy Presence. You have filled your left brain to the brim with puzzles upon puzzles that lead to nowhere. This is your way of protecting yourself from the Truth. It is the Human Way. The Truth is not some 'thing' to be afraid of. However, when the Truth becomes brighter, it can cause many to shrink away. For you feel that you are not worthy of such Presence. For you feel guilt, remorse, fear, and pain. The Truth does indeed set you free, and it is your choice to hide, or to let the light inside of you come out from behind the shadows that your ego has placed before you. Have the courage to take a peek at the wonders that life is holding out to you. Take baby steps if it makes you feel better. Ask questions if you have them. The Holy Presence of Now is not fleeting. It is always here, but the human way is to completely miss it, as you spend so much time in the past and in the future. Take note of those moments in which you know that you have chosen to experience this

Presence, the moments when you have chosen not to turn back and take a look. Take note of those moments when you have chosen to not worry about the future. When you step into the Holy Presence, even if for a few seconds, you will know you have been home. You have the ability to be in this Holy Presence right now. You may go about your daily activities and be in this Presence. It is only a matter of 'how?' When you have been so used to living in the past, and jumping into the future, how do you become aware of this moment? Become aware of simply all that you do, and make a choice to BE fully aware. If you notice that you are aware, you have just taken that step, you have been inside of the experience of the Holy Presence of Now. This Presence is your essence. It is who you are.

Sticks & Stones

'Sticks and stones may break my bones but words will never hurt me.'

Countless times we have heard this phrase chanted, mostly by children. This mantra was given to them so that they could overcome the effects of would be bullying.

When a person says something hurtful on purpose towards another human being, this is a sign of their own inner insecurities and weakness. In order to make themselves feel more powerful, in order to raise their ego up, they must gain control over your emotions. If they can see that they have hurt you, their power has risen. If, however, you do not show any outward sign of emotional response to their words, their balloon has then deflated.

Well, that takes care of part of the issue. The other part is what happens when those words actually do hurt? Once you've successfully deflated that ego balloon of the other person by not showing any outward emotional response, you then have to take care of the pain that it actually caused you. Pushing it inwards is not a good idea.

We all know people who bottle up their emotions and at some point, the bottle explodes into fits of anger, temper tantrums, and in countless other ways that serve no one.

You must let the pain flow out, like water running through a screen. You must be the observer of these feelings. Watch them, let them run their short course through, and say good-bye to them. There is no point in keeping them within you, for the words that have caused you pain will only live as long as you keep their memories alive in your thoughts.

So one lesson we can take from this is that we need to be extremely cautious with our words, whether they be spoken or written. We, as Spiritual Beings, are using these physical bodies, dressing up in them to play and dream and live and experience.

We have been given many useful tools to use in this world. In the case of words, we have been given mouths to speak with, eyes to read with, ears to listen with, and fingers to write with.

In every case of written or spoken expression, words are extremely powerful!

You can see the power of words in some of our great historical presences.

For instance:

"There is nothing to fear, but fear itself" by FDR

"Ask not what your country can do for you, ask what you can do for your country" by JFK

"And so I tell you, keep on asking, and you will receive what you ask for. Keep on seeking, and you will find. Keep on knocking, and the door will be opened to you. For everyone who asks, receives. Everyone who seeks finds. And to everyone who knocks, the door will be opened." By Jesus

"We must be the change we wish to see" by Ghandi

Use your words wisely and lovingly to all within your path. In the same way, use your words wisely and lovingly towards yourself.

Tao Te Ching Verse 2

When people see some things as beautiful,
other things become ugly.
When people see some things as good,
other things become bad.

Being and non-being create each other.
Difficult and easy support each other.
Long and short define each other.
High and low depend on each other.
Before and after follow each other.

Therefore the Master
acts without doing anything
and teaches without saying anything.

Things arise and she lets them come;
things disappear and she lets them go.

She has but doesn't possess,
acts but doesn't expect.

When her work is done, she forgets it.
That is why it lasts forever.

Interpretation from my perspective:

We create separations in our minds, opposites, polarities, ,
because we use judgment to place value upon things. We can
only identify beautiful because we've identified ugly. We can
only identify good because we've identified bad. This is true
for all things that we place opposite values on. You cannot be
part of the whole, because that would imply again, a
separation, a duality. Therefore, we are the Whole. It's a
paradox but we live it while roaming this physical plane. It is
possible to be in the paradox and not be of the paradox. We can
be in the world but not of it. Be in the world knowing that there
is Unity, that there is no reason to judge anything and place
value upon the things of the world, because all things are the

same, all things come from one. Be inside of the stillness. See God in all things. Whether something has been judged as beautiful or ugly matters not, whether a person has been identified as good or bad matters not, the sun still shines upon all things, without favor.

The Art of Allowing

Depending on how you look at life, at one time or another you have encountered a problem of some sort. Sometimes these problems seem small, and sometimes these problems seem huge. It really all depends on your own perception of things.

An issue arises. The issue could have been simple, but we chose to delve deeper. Note that I said we chose to delve deeper. We chose to pick it apart, we chose to scrutinize it, we chose to judge it, and then what happened? We made a mountain out of a mole hill. Some problems actually get to be really hairy BECAUSE we've thought about them too much; we've made them materialize into something real.

We don't have to get stuck in these problems. We don't have to always trudge uphill through them; we don't have to sink into them as if we're suddenly standing in quick sand. We can allow ourselves to LEAP over them.

I've had what you could call 'rough times' in areas of my life, in the past. Note that I said, in the past. The thing about the past is that it's all gone now, it's all over. The past will absolutely not repeat itself because I have learned my lessons from there. If I didn't learn the lessons I was supposed to learn, then I'm sure the past would creep back in. But I've moved on. I can look and say, 'hey, I made it past that'. And so, whenever a problem seemingly tries to arise in my day to day life, I say, [wait a minute, this doesn't have to be a problem...after all, I've gotten past all the others. I can just LEAP over this one because after a while, it won't be there anymore.' I can just allow whatever the perceived problem is to be and to flow in and right back out. However, if I resist against this flow, if I push back, if I fight it, the perceived problem/issue will stay there, stuck in an endless loop.

Try to be in the flow, and allow it to be there. Be in it, feel it as it moves through and on out.

The act of allowing is an art. We have set ourselves up to struggle against things that come into our life, but that can all be changed now.

To practice the art of allowing is an act of creatorship.

Tao Te Ching Verse 1

The tao that can be told
is not the eternal Tao
The name that can be named
is not the eternal Name.

The unnamable is the eternally real.
Naming is the origin
of all particular things.

Free from desire, you realize the mystery.
Caught in desire, you see only the manifestations.

Yet mystery and manifestations
arise from the same source.
This source is called darkness.

Darkness within darkness.
The gateway to all understanding

Tao. This to me means the Universal, Invisible, All That Is. The Tao is where everything comes from, yet, remains unseen, it is indeed Eternal. We have given it the name of Tao and other names, yet, the eternal name is unknown. There is no name for the invisible. However, the un-nameable IS eternally real. Most of us go through life needing to see to believe in something, however, whether you believe or not, it IS real. Once you let go and allow your life to unfold, you will begin to 'feel' and 'know' the Tao, you will begin to experience it, the mystery. When you are focused only on the want or the desire to fill up your life with things in the physical, material world, you only SEE the physical, material world. The mystery and the physical things all come from the same place. There is nothing that is separate.

Awestruck

Whenever I see a shooting star, I am awestruck. I guess it's because it reminds me of how large and mysterious the Universe really is. I've never seen the Northern Lights in person, but I can imagine that they are gorgeous. There are so many beautiful things that our eyes are able to behold. Is there any person whose eyes do not widen when they seem something so wonderful?

Then there is Science. Science can take the mystery right out of the mysterious. Or can it?

There are explanations for shooting stars and for the Northern Lights, and for many different things that produce a sense of wonder inside of us. But is it the full explanation? Probably not. Even Scientists change their ideas on things every so often.

This is because the world outside is in a constant state of motion. Things on the outside never stay the same.

The inner world, the world that lives within us, is much the same. It feels as if we are in constant motion. Things are ever changing. Our lives unfold in a series of pages, as in a book. One day is not the same as another. We may try to hold onto something, to try to make it 'not change', but that rarely works. If we don't allow things to change, we will be stuck in the same place, having the same ideas for years and years.

Be awestruck by the wonders of your inner world.

I must add that there IS one thing that does not ever change, for there is no need. That one thing is the essence of you, rather, your soul. Your soul has been and will always be. Your soul waits for discovery, in a state of no-thing, waiting for you to tap into it.

Release the Hold of the Mind

Through every event that takes place in your day, you have a choice. Each moment contains an event, a choice. You can either engage in those things that cause upheaval in your life, or you can identify what's about to take place, and stop yourself from engaging, resulting in a feeling of quiet calm. When things are about to happen, sometimes we miss the signs, and other times, we can catch ourselves. If you begin to set the intent to catch yourself, watch what happens with your life, as it rolls out into play.

What you are about to read is meant to challenge you to become an active participant in your life. A lot of the things listed below we do without even thinking about them. This is the hold that the mind has on us. If we can release ourselves from it's grasp, or at least begin to see the grasp it has on us, we can become more conscious of our Present moment.

Let go of taking things personally.

The common human error that we make is that everything said has something to do with us. Other people's lives, however, do not actually revolve around us. If someone makes a comment that unintentionally could hurt our feelings, we don't have to let that happen. Realize that many people just don't know what the effect of a comment or situation may have upon the other person. Don't take things personally. Release yourself of this need.

Let go of the need to be right about all things.

Do you find yourself having to prove to others how right you are? Why? What good does it do to make yourself right and someone else wrong? Does your way have to be the only way? Realize that other people may have something significant to offer, and let them speak. Release yourself of the need to do this.

Let go of being competitive.

What is the need for competition? Do you have to always be the 'winner'? Realize that even if you lose in a game, it's perfectly acceptable. You don't have to get angry or sulk if you don't 'win'. Release yourself of the need to always win.

Let go of needing to be 'like' others.

Do you have to have what everyone else has? Why? Realize that you are perfect just the way you are, with just what you have right now. Release yourself of the need to be like others.

Let go of the need to be looked upon positively by others.

Do you always worry about what other people make think of you? Don't worry about it. You cannot please everyone, and you won't. Release yourself of the need to be looked up positively by others.

Let go of the idea that you have someone to blame for what happens in your life.

Do you blame others for what is happening in your life right now, or how your life is turning out? Realize that you are the creator of your life. There is no one to blame. Everything happens in perfect timing and for reasons sometimes that you can't see right now. Release yourself of the need to blame others.

Let go of the past and the future.

Are you constantly living in the past, or worrying about the future? If so, this can cause a state of unease, panic, and anxiety. Focus on what is going on right now. When you release yourself from the ties that bind you to the past and the future, you release yourself from the entanglement of stress.

Let go of complaints.

Why complain about things? Ask yourself what good it does for you right now to complain. It doesn't do anything really. It normally builds upon itself until you have gotten yourself so angry that you don't know how to get out of the irritation. Release yourself from the need to complain.

Let go of the need to gossip.

Ever find yourself in a situation where you join in on the he said/she said game? This eventually causes tension not just to yourself, but to those whom you have just included in the gossip game. Release yourself from the need to gossip.

Let go of the need to be in drama-mode.

Sometimes people are addicted to drama. If there isn't drama, something feels amiss. You may have grown so used to being inside of a drama, that you feel lost without it. Being with-out drama brings a space of nothingness. Incredibly, if you stay inside and just be in the nothing-ness, there is peace. Release yourself of the need to be in drama-mode.

The Locator

I found a show called 'The Locator' a couple of weeks ago, and once I watched one episode I couldn't stop watching the other ones. If you haven't seen this show, let me tell you a little bit about it so that you can fully understand what I'm going to be writing about. In short, 'The Locator' is Troy Dunn. In 1990, Troy helped his own mother, who was adopted as a baby, locate her own biological family. That single event inspired Troy to help people reunite with long lost friends and family members.

Whenever I watch an episode of this show, I have found myself literally crying like a baby. Tears of sadness roll down my face as I listen to their personal stories, most often of sacrifice. As you get to the middle of the show, the tears become tears of happiness as these people finally re-unite. What Troy does is re-unite them in a surprising way, where one of them doesn't know that they are finding who they were looking for.

So I was lying in bed, ready to go to sleep, reflecting, and a comparison began to arise.

Some of us walk around in our lives, always feeling that there is something missing. We try desperately to fill that emptiness with a variety of things, such as people, food, cars, clothes, jewelry, homes, etc. Yet, after a while, the emptiness returns. We find that there just isn't anything that truly makes that hole inside disappear.

But you see, we have our own 'Locator'. This Locator has always been with us. We've just overlooked it. Our Locator does things to get our attention, and sometimes these things are subtle, and other times, our Locator hits us right on the head! Even then, we may not listen. But one day, we find that we just can't ignore our Locator any longer. So, we begin a different kind of journey than we've ever embarked on before.

Ultimately, we find that in our quietest moments, we can actually hear our Locator! We begin to listen, we begin to experience, and we begin to feel!

By following the guidance of our Locator, we are led Home. We realize that Home isn't a far out destination, Home has always been with us, and with this realization comes a deep peace, a sense of belonging, and there is no longer any emptiness. There is a release of emotion when we find our Home again.

Much like I described above, we have a reunion like we've never had before.

Find your Locator, you don't have to look very far, and most of all, follow It's guidance, and you will begin to remember who you are.

Expansion

I have changed from who I once was. This is part of life. Who I was 5 years ago, is completely different from who I am today. You could ask me one question then, and get one answer, and ask me the same question today, and get a completely different answer. 5 years ago, I wasn't on the Spiritual Path that I am on today. There have always been parts of me moving me in the direction that I am going, but the past 5 years have been spent on an inner journey, so to speak.

Spiritually speaking, growth and expansion are continuously approaching me. This happens because I have asked for it. I know that expansion is my purpose here on Earth. My purpose is to expand my Self by listening to the Divine presence within me.

How did I come to that knowledge? I didn't come to that knowledge by reading it in a book, or because someone told me that this is so. I came to this knowledge by connecting with the part of me that doesn't live in the physical dimension, the part of me that lives within the Super Consciousness, and this would be my Higher Self. I use the term Higher to only create an image, but the term Higher does not mean above or better. My Higher Self is the part of me that is connected fully and completely and truly to Source.

We all have this Higher Self. When we listen, we are given instantaneous knowledge on a deep level. Connecting to the Higher Self is much easier that most think. However, it does take a certain amount of patience in the beginning. We have fast paced lives, and if we are not willing to create the space for ourselves, not willing to slow down and sit in silence, we will not find that connection.

Polarities

Do you only embrace the positive, do you only embrace the light? I see a lot of people only holding onto the Light and desperately trying to push the darkness and the negativity out. I see the caption 'we are one' everywhere.

The idea that 'we are one' is not lost on me. In fact, it is one of my biggest truths.

However, you see, to have the truth of Oneness, we must understand, really we must 'know' and 'feel' inside of us what Love is. Love is what encompasses all things. Love is a field of energy, and Love holds the vibrations of duality here. Love does not judge the way that we judge. For example: good/bad, pretty/ugly, positive/negative, etc. Because Love does not judge, we must understand that Light/Darkness go together.

If you only embrace the Light, there is no balance. Embrace the Light as well as the darkness, embrace the positive as well as the negative, embrace the good as well as the bad. For in all of these things, in all of these polarities is One Vibration, Love.

Is Meditation Important?

From my perspective, meditation is one of the most important tools that you can use to have all of your questions answered. If you have a question, the answer is already there. All of the answers are already there, waiting, inside of you to be unwrapped, by you and only you.

There are many ways given on how to meditate. You can find these ways given in a multitude of books and online sources. However, you will have to develop your own way of meditation as time goes by, to do it in the way that honors your own experience.

If you are one of those that don't have the patience, then you are likely one of those who needs meditation the most. It provides a space for you to 'have' more patience, a space for you to 'have' more peace in your life.

Our lives are filled with busy work. Everything moves at such a fast pace. Taking the time to slow yourself down and sit in a place of quietness, or taking a walk in nature, is like giving yourself a much needed spa treatment, and its completely free of charge.

ABOUT THE AUTHOR

LESLIE SMITH, B.MSC.

Leslie is an author of spiritual and metaphysical titles, a freelance & e-book writer, and has contributed to several online publications. Additionally, she is a philosopher, visionary, and working on her Doctorate in Metaphysics. Her latest project is a spiritual self help compilation which will be published in January of 2009.

Made in the USA
Lexington, KY
01 November 2012